ABOVE: *Afternoons are frequently taken up with public engagements. The Queen, who is patron of the King Edward VII Hospital for Officers, smiles at nursing staff as she opens a new wing. The Royal Family and their staff are all treated at this hospital.*

TOP: *The Prime Minister has a close working relationship with The Queen and keeps her informed of government business. She is seen here with John Major.*

LEFT: *The Queen begins her working day at her desk, when she has to deal with much correspondence and important affairs of State. Even here, at her country home in Sandringham, she must keep up to date with events.*

# Constitutional Monarch

ABOVE: *The Maundy Thursday Service is a historic ceremony, during which The Queen presents specially minted coins to elderly members of the congregation.*

ABOVE RIGHT: *Trooping the Colour takes place on Horse Guards Parade in June each year. The regimental flag was originally displayed to the soldiers for instant recognition in battle.*

OPPOSITE BELOW LEFT: *Membership of the ancient Order of the Garter is a personal gift from the Sovereign and is a distinguished honour.*

As a constitutional monarch, The Queen's powers are in theory awesome. The Prime Minister and Cabinet are strictly speaking her servants and all government work is carried out in her name – 'On Her Majesty's Service'. She is head of the judiciary, Commander-in-Chief of all the armed forces and the temporal head of the established Church of England. The Queen could sell all the ships in the navy or disband the army. It is in her name that war is declared and it is her personal ambassadors who represent the United Kingdom abroad and it is to her Court of St James's that ambassadors from other countries are accredited. In practice, of course, all these decisions are taken in true democratic style by the elected government of the day: in effect The Queen reigns but does not rule.

As Defender of the Faith Her Majesty is responsible for setting an example to her people. When she was anointed with holy oils at her coronation, Her Majesty accepted a sacred trust, one which she believes she must hold for life.

The Queen has no power in a political sense yet she is an integral part of the parliamentary system. Each year at the State Opening of Parliament she reads the speech outlining her government's proposals for the coming session. No bill becomes law until Royal Assent has been granted, and decisions under Royal Prerogative receive her approval at meetings of the Privy Council. A former Prime Minister of the United Kingdom, Lord Callaghan of Cardiff, once remarked, 'No practising politician could possibly hope to be more deeply and widely informed about domestic, Commonwealth and international affairs than The Queen. She has sources of information available to nobody else.'

It is The Queen who makes formal appointments to all the important offices of State and in the armed services and

Church of England. She also confers peerages, knighthoods and other honours.

Yet it is as a figurehead that The Queen is seen by most of her subjects, never more so than when she takes part in the spectacular ceremonial and pageantry associated with royalty, such as Trooping the Colour on the occasion of her Official Birthday every June.

In November The Queen leads other members of the Royal Family in paying tribute to the dead of two World Wars and numerous smaller conflicts at the annual Remembrance Service at The Cenotaph in Whitehall. It is an occasion of great sadness when the Sovereign publicly shares with her people their private grief.

On a lighter note, Her Majesty patronises fashionable events such as Royal Ascot and the Derby. Watching her own horses compete adds greatly to the excitement.

ABOVE: *An open landau conveys The Queen and the Duke of Edinburgh to the Ascot Races at Windsor.*

LEFT: *Overseas tours form an important part of The Queen's itinerary and are generally made for diplomatic reasons. She is seen here in the USA.*

# The Queen and the Commonwealth

SCIENCE WORL

ABOVE: *Vancouver provides a warm welcome to Her Majesty, who pays regular visits to Canada. The Mayor has escorted her around an exhibition of world science.*

OPPOSITE BELOW: *The people of Antigua are thrilled to be able to have a word with The Queen during an informal walkabout. Several of the Caribbean islands belong to the Commonwealth and their affairs are followed with keen interest by Her Majesty.*

Elizabeth II is recognised as Queen or Head of the Commonwealth by no fewer than 50 countries varying in size from the continent of Australia to tiny island independencies in the South Pacific whose populations are less than those of an outer London Borough. She is, however, Head of State of only 17 of these countries in which she is represented by a Governor-General. Altogether the Commonwealth has a total population of 1,200 million, or a quarter of the world's people.

It is freely admitted in royal circles that The Queen believes her role in the Commonwealth to be just as important as her position as Queen of the United Kingdom and many of her friends in Commonwealth countries are emphatic about the part she plays. A former

Secretary-General of the Commonwealth explained that The Queen occupies a unique position, which is unique because of who she is, not simply because of the title she holds. He said, 'She is the most experienced Head of State in the world and she regards many of the Commonwealth leaders as personal friends and all of them, without exception, look to her for guidance and advice.' It is also important to remember that five of the Commonwealth countries are monarchies in their own right: Brunei, Lesotho, Malaysia, Swaziland and Tonga.

The Commonwealth is a free association of independent states which are former British colonies. Membership is entirely voluntary and The Queen was appointed Head of the Commonwealth by

common consent, not just because she is Queen. She makes one official visit to a Commonwealth country at least once every year and she also receives reciprocal visits from their Heads of State, and broadcasts a radio and television message to them all on Christmas Day.

Prime Ministers of Commonwealth countries have direct access to The Queen without having to go through the British Foreign Office or any other agency, and it is a right jealously guarded on both sides. The secretariat is based in London at Marlborough House, the former home of Queen Mary, which has been placed at the Commonwealth's permanent disposal by Queen Elizabeth II.

ABOVE: *The traditional art of finger-painting is demonstrated to The Queen and Prince Philip during their tour of Malaysia.*

ABOVE LEFT: *In Kuala Lumpur a special ceremony is mounted to welcome The Queen. Her Majesty fosters close working relationships with Commonwealth leaders, who have a considerable respect for her. The fact that The Queen is politically neutral, combined with her vast experience of affairs of State, means that she is an invaluable source of information and advice.*

# Royal Travel

Elizabeth II is without doubt the most widely travelled monarch of all time. Since her accession in February 1952 she has visited more countries, met more people and shaken hands with more of her own subjects than all her predecessors combined.

There are three main departments within the Royal Household to deal with the travel requirements of the Royal Family: The Queen's Flight, which has responsibility not only for providing its own aircraft when required, but also for the arrangements when a member of the Royal Family is travelling by commercial airline; the Royal Mews, whose head, the Crown Equerry, looks after all transport by road, that is royal limousine (there are five State Rolls-Royces, the only cars in Britain permitted to drive on public roads without displaying registration plates), private car, on horseback or in one of the State carriages; and the Royal Yacht *Britannia*, which is an independent Royal Navy command, and is the only ship in the world whose captain has the distinction of being an admiral. There is one other method of transport used by The Queen and her family and that is the Royal Train which is owned and operated by British Rail which charges the Privy Purse (the treasury of the Royal Household) for all royal journeys.

OPPOSITE LEFT: *The Royal Yacht* Britannia *provides a comfortable means of transport. Its elegant interior is often used for the entertainment of foreign guests when members of the Royal Family are making visits abroad.*

OPPOSITE RIGHT: *The Princess of Wales waves goodbye to the crowds at Oxford before returning home in a helicopter of The Queen's Flight.*

RIGHT: *The Royal Train has brought Her Majesty safely to Swansea.*

ABOVE: *Even the royal corgis are experienced air passengers of The Queen's Flight.*

LEFT CENTRE: *One of the five Rolls-Royces owned by The Queen. She waves happily as she arrives at Powis Castle in Wales.*

BELOW: *An open landau allows the public to have a perfect view of Her Majesty as she leaves Buckingham Palace for Trooping the Colour.*

The Queen's Flight is based at RAF Benson in Oxfordshire where 180 personnel fly and service the BAe 146 medium-range jet aircraft and the Westland Wessex helicopters. The aircraft are easily recognisable by their distinctive colour schemes of bright red and white, while the helicopters are all painted red. They are often seen over London as they land and take off from the gardens behind Buckingham Palace. Prince Philip, the Prince of Wales and the Duke of York are all qualified pilots.

*Britannia* was launched in 1953, the year of the coronation, and her captain is a member of the Royal Household. When the Royal Family is on board all commands are given by silent signal and soft shoes are worn by the crew in order to give as much peace and privacy as possible.

The Royal Mews at Buckingham Palace contains the 30 horses used in State processions and in the everyday routine of delivering official documents around London, plus the magnificent collection of State coaches and carriages. Of the five Rolls-Royce limousines in the Mews, the most important is a Phantom VI which has a removable outer roof covering. Whenever The Queen is travelling in one of her official cars a solid-silver mascot depicting St George and the Dragon is fixed to the bonnet.

# Royalty Entertains

ABOVE: *Some of the 9,000 guests invited to a Garden Party at Buckingham Palace. Only a few can be presented to royalty on each occasion, but all can enjoy tea served in marquees on the sweeping lawns.*

OPPOSITE BELOW LEFT: *The Prince and Princess of Wales frequently have private dinner parties at their home in Kensington Palace. Guests might include key people from the business world or the professions, as well as personal friends.*

The Queen is the country's official hostess entertaining, on behalf of her people, guests from all over the world. There are no fewer than 80 functions held at Buckingham Palace alone every year ranging from the three Garden Parties, to each of which some 9,000 guests are invited, down to small informal luncheons where the guest list runs to only about eight people. Perhaps the most elegant of all events in the royal year is the Diplomatic Reception held in November, when members of the Diplomatic Corps based in London are invited to Buckingham Palace to meet The Queen and her family. All the magnificent State rooms are open and every guest is wearing full formal evening dress or national costume and decorations. It is an occasion for diamond tiaras and these, together with the ladies' colourful ball-gowns, create a glittering spectacle.

If a foreign Head of State has been invited to Buckingham Palace, The Queen, as the perfect hostess, personally inspects the Belgian Suite to ensure her guests' comfort. A State Banquet will be given in the State Ballroom in honour of the visitor. In between these splendid celebrations, numerous less formal lunches, dinners and cocktail parties are held.

When the Queen attends a performance at the Royal Opera House, Covent Garden, she takes her own food and drink. Footmen prepare a light supper in the private dining room adjoining the Royal Box, with china, cutlery and linen brought from the Palace for the occasion.

Other members of the Royal Family are also generous hosts and hostesses, with an invitation to one of Queen Elizabeth the Queen Mother's lunches being highly sought after. Her Majesty's London home, Clarence House, is the most informal of all royal residences and in the summer she likes her guests to join her in the garden

LEFT: *Foreign Heads of State are received in grand style. Here The Queen and her guest, the President of Nigeria, are driven to Buckingham Palace in the 1902 State Landau.*

BELOW: *While moored off the coast of Malaysia, the Royal Yacht* Britannia *offers a gracious venue for the entertainment of the Yang di-Pertuan Agong and his wife.*

where they dine under the plane trees – and where they can hear what people passing on the other side of the boundary wall are saying!

Princess Margaret, who lives in Kensington Palace, gives perhaps the most sophisticated parties, with guests from the world of the theatre and the arts. The evenings rarely end before midnight and sometimes the hostess entertains her guests by singing selections from some of the most popular shows, while accompanying herself on the piano.

An invitation to dinner at the home of the Prince and Princess of Wales means an evening of elegance, charm and superb cuisine. Champagne is offered on arrival; the finest wines are served with the meal (even though both the Prince and his wife barely drink themselves) and the only rules are that everyone must enjoy themselves – but no smoking! Prince Charles refuses to allow it in his home.

# Royal Patronage

RIGHT: *The Princess Royal, tirelessly helping to raise funds and support for the Save the Children Fund, attends one such event in Cambridge.*

RIGHT: *Using sign language to communicate, the Princess of Wales shows how earnestly she takes her role as patron of the deaf and dumb.*

makes herself available to visit their branches or lend her support to fund-raising events.

Prince Philip has involved himself in many charities since he became a member of the Royal Family in 1947 and in doing so he has created a special place for himself in the life of the nation. The Duke of Edinburgh's Award Scheme was his own idea to 'encourage in the individual the spirit of voluntary service, self-reliance and perseverance, a sense of responsibility and the pursuit of hobbies and other leisure activities'. Many thousands of young people have taken part in the Scheme and these days Prince Edward is becoming more and more involved with the organisation, carrying out a number of duties on his father's behalf. Another of Prince Philip's most active interests is the World Wide Fund for Nature, for which he travels regularly and extensively;

Every member of the Royal Family is involved in working for charitable causes and inevitably some have become more closely identified with one in particular. The Princess Royal's name is practically synonymous with the Save the Children Fund, of which she has been President since 1969. It was her first public appointment and she has worked tirelessly for its aims ever since. She travels throughout the Third World promoting the Fund's work and she has become an expert in the problems of child care and famine relief. But she is also associated with many other charities including one very dear to her heart, Riding for the Disabled. As a former Olympic horsewoman, she brings a special understanding to this voluntary body and

LEFT: *The Prince of Wales, eager to encourage business ventures, especially among young people, appreciates Scottish crafts in Leith.*

CENTRE: *Prince Edward helps to promote a scheme initiated by his father, the Duke of Edinburgh's Award, in Battersea Park, London.*

BOTTOM: *As President of the World Wide Fund for Nature, Prince Philip paid a visit to Chitwan Park, Nepal, where he admired the elephants. He is dedicated to protecting the natural world from commercial exploitation and pollution.*

he became its President in 1981.

The Prince and Princess of Wales like to refer to their various charities as their 'Family of Organisations'. The three main charities associated with Prince Charles are: The Prince's Trust, founded in 1976 to help young people develop their potential, Business in the Community and the Prince's Advisory Group on Disability. The Princess of Wales is actively involved with charities dealing with deafness, old age, drugs and drink dependency, marriage counselling, children and childbirth. She has become an expert communicator and is equally at home with infants and young adults or octogenarians.

Princess Margaret is also closely involved with several charities concerning children's welfare, including Dr Barnardo's and the NSPCC.

Now into her tenth decade, Queen Elizabeth the Queen Mother is still active in the charities she supports with over 300 organisations bearing her name as president, patron or member. Her work for the National Trust and the RSPCA spans well over half a century, and small charities like the Injured Jockeys' Fund reflect her special interests.

13

# Leaders of Fashion

Her Majesty the Queen.

for Trooping the Colour 1988

ABOVE: *Elegant designs by Ian Thomas. The one on the left shows that The Queen prefers to have two dresses to go with one coat. The pink outfit brightened up the dull weather at the Braemar Games.*

RIGHT: *The colour of this evening dress makes a stunning contrast with the Duchess of York's red hair.*

The ladies in the Royal Family all have one purpose in mind when they come to choose their clothes: it is to ensure that everything they wear does credit to the family and reflects favourably on the British fashion industry for which they are unofficial but highly regarded representatives.

The Queen's wardrobe plays an important part in her public life and three designers share the responsibility of providing Her Majesty with her clothes. They are the House of Hartnell, which also designs for the Queen Mother and which

many occasions and climates, so dresses that might be perfect for a spring day in Scotland may not be what is required for a hot and humid evening in Singapore.

The Princess of Wales is arguably the most fashionable woman in the world and her style is emulated by young women of her generation in many countries. Her hats are made by John Boyd and Freddie Fox and she alone is said to have saved the British millinery trade. Young British designers create her outfits, including Bruce Oldfield, Catherine Walker, Murray Arbeid and David Emanuel who, with his wife Elizabeth, was responsible for making the Princess's wedding dress in 1981. Both she and her sister-in-law the Duchess of York are regarded as trend-setters and while the Duchess has a more flamboyant style, favouring striking colours and eye-catching designs, the Princess of Wales emphasizes her slim silhouette with neat classical lines.

LEFT: *This softly gathered, shimmering material gives the Princess of Wales a slightly Oriental air.*

CENTRE: *A daring dress, toned down by the Princess's velvet jacket.*

BELOW: *Pastel shades and gentle flowing lines are the Queen Mother's style.*

made The Queen's wedding dress, Sir Hardy Amies who was knighted for his services to the Sovereign, and the latest designer Ian Thomas, who originally worked for Hartnell. There is friendly rivalry but no jealousy among these three because The Queen may change her clothes three times a day at home and up to five times a day when abroad, so there is plenty of work for them all.

If The Queen is planning an extended overseas tour the proposed itinerary will be sent to each of the designers many months beforehand. They will then submit drawings from which The Queen makes her choice. The dresses and suits of each designer are kept in separate closets, so that when one of them is attending The Queen for a fitting, he cannot see his competitors' work. To make sure that The Queen knows which hat goes with which dress, Ian Thomas always pins a small piece of fabric inside the hat band. There is one factor that all royal designers must take into account – the clothes must not crease! They must also be suitable for

ABOVE: *Princess Margaret has chosen a romantic, floating dress for this gala occasion. The bodice is intricately embroidered in silver and the sleeves are stiffened to stand away from the neckline.*

LEFT: *The Queen prefers close-fitting hats, so that they are less likely to be knocked sideways when climbing in and out of cars.*

# Royal Jewellery

ABOVE: *Oblong sapphires surrounded by diamonds feature in the necklace and earrings given to The Queen by her father, George VI, as a wedding gift. The tiara was later made to match.*

ABOVE RIGHT: *The Duchess of York looks radiant in these diamonds, which were personal gifts from The Queen and Prince Philip.*

RIGHT: *'Granny's tiara' was a wedding gift from Queen Mary. The other jewels are the Cambridge emerald earrings and 'Ladies of India' necklace.*

OPPOSITE BELOW: *Princess Margaret first wore the Poltimore tiara on her wedding day in 1960.*

Jewellery is a vital part of the royal wardrobe and The Queen owns the finest private collection in the world. It has been amassed over many years in a variety of ways, with many of the most valuable items being handed down from generation to generation. The basis of the present royal collection was established by Queen Victoria, who spent an enormous sum of money on jewellery, and the most famous jewels that the Royal Family wears today, the Koh-i-noor, the diamond collet necklace and the Indian regal tiara, were all acquired in her reign.

Queen Mary had a reputation for being the most avid collector of jewellery and even today the brooch made from the fabulous Cullinan Diamond, said to be the most valuable in the world, is known within the family as 'Granny's Chips'.

A significant number of pieces within the modern royal collection has been acquired in the form of gifts from Heads of State of countries visited by The Queen and her family, or even by private individuals. In 1947 a Canadian millionaire presented Princess Elizabeth with the world's largest pink diamond as a wedding present, and in the coronation year it was made up into a daffodil flower brooch.

The ladies in the Royal Family have

always passed on certain items of jewellery to the next generation and the Princess of Wales's first great jewel was a tiara of lovers' knots of diamonds from which hang 19 perfect drop pearls. This was a wedding present from The Queen, who had worn the tiara herself in the 1950s, and she, in turn, had inherited it from Queen Mary, who had it made in 1914. Another of the Princess of Wales's priceless items of jewellery is a sapphire and diamond necklace, together with matching earrings and bracelet, which were presented to her by the Sultan of Oman during the Gulf tour of 1986.

Privately, both the Princess of Wales and the Duchess of York prefer to wear costume jewellery known as 'fabulous fakes'. These are copies which are so realistic that they are almost indistinguishable from the real thing. Most are modern pieces such as the 'diamond'

RIGHT: *The fabulous necklace with crescent earrings presented to the Princess of Wales by the Sultan of Oman. The tiara is a Spencer heirloom.*

BELOW: *The Queen Mother wears the honeycomb tiara made up from diamonds given to Edward VII by the well-known diamond merchants de Beers.*

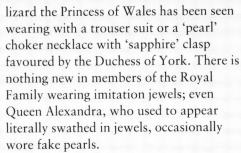

lizard the Princess of Wales has been seen wearing with a trouser suit or a 'pearl' choker necklace with 'sapphire' clasp favoured by the Duchess of York. There is nothing new in members of the Royal Family wearing imitation jewels; even Queen Alexandra, who used to appear literally swathed in jewels, occasionally wore fake pearls.

Six jewellers hold the Royal Warrant but only one, Garrard, is known as *the* Crown Jewellers. This is because they not only make royal jewellery, they also look after the Crown Jewels, which are not the private property of the Sovereign. Most of them have been supplying the Royal Family for generations but one, Andrew Grima, was awarded his Royal Warrant only in 1970 after making a number of spectacular diamond brooches for The Queen. Two of them, Collingwood and Garrard, enjoy a very special relationship because they make wedding rings for all the royal brides from the same seam of Welsh gold.

# The Family Firm

King George VI once described the Royal Family as 'the Family Firm' and the Duke of Edinburgh has said that living at Buckingham Palace is like 'living over the shop'. Public interest in the Royal Family has grown to such an extent that in any one year its members receive thousands of invitations to attend various functions, make speeches or simply to grace an event with their presence. The Queen is the one with the greatest workload, carrying out more than 500 engagements a year at home and abroad, but these days the burden has been spread a little as other members of the family take on various commitments.

The Duke of Edinburgh acts as patron or president of many important organisations and devotes much of his time to the conservation of the countryside and the state of the environment, both in

ABOVE: *Meticulous planning is essential months in advance of engagements. The Princess of Wales discusses the finer points with a Lady-in-Waiting, Anne Beckwith-Smith, while Prince Charles adds his comments.*

RIGHT: *The Duke and Duchess of York spent some time with handicapped children during their visit to Australia in the year of the Bicentenary. Here they meet a boy who has been blind since birth.*

RIGHT CENTRE: *Even Prince William, seen here with his mother, has begun his royal duties, much to the delight of onlookers, eager to shake his hand.*

LEFT: *Smiling children greet The Queen in Southampton. Her natural manner and genuine interest in people help them to overcome their shyness.*

BELOW LEFT: *The Princess Royal took over from her grandmother as Chancellor of London University in 1980. Clad in her honorary academic robes, she takes part in a degree ceremony at the Royal Albert Hall.*

Britain and overseas. In addition he holds a large number of appointments in the armed services.

The other members of the Royal Family also have a heavy programme of engagements and every effort is made by the Household to ensure that they do not duplicate their duties or that, geographically, their paths do not cross. As both Princess Margaret and the Princess of Wales are keenly interested in the arts, the former concentrates on the Royal Ballet as its President, while the Princess of Wales has accepted the role of Patron of the Welsh National Opera.

The Queen Mother was Chancellor of London University until she was 80, when she passed on this role to her granddaughter the Princess Royal. In 1978 the Queen Mother was appointed Lord Warden of the Cinque Ports. She considered this a special privilege as she was the first woman to hold this office.

As for Prince Charles, he has so many calls on his time that his programme is worked out a full year in advance.

# In Uniform

ABOVE: *The Duke of York, an officer in the Royal Navy, received his wings as a helicopter pilot in 1981. He chats with two young ratings in Sydney.*

RIGHT: *Prince Charles wears his uniform of Captain in the Royal Navy during his tour of Czechoslovakia. He is accompanied by the President Vàclav Havel.*

The British Royal Family has always had close associations with all branches of the armed forces. The Queen is Commander-in-Chief of all three services, the Army, the Royal Navy and the Royal Air Force and other members of the family hold important appointments in one or more of the services. The only event at which Her Majesty has appeared in uniform, however, was the annual Sovereign's Birthday Parade (Trooping the Colour) when she rode her horse Burmese to review her foot guards, accompanied by Prince Philip as Colonel of the Coldstream Guards, Prince Charles as Colonel of the Welsh Guards and the Duke of Kent, Colonel of the Scots Guards. However, this practice ended in 1986 and Her Majesty now drives to the parade in a carriage wearing day dress. During the Second World War she served as a commissioned officer in the Auxiliary

Territorial Service with the serial number 230873 which, like all service men and women, she said she would remember for the rest of her life.

The Duke of Edinburgh was also a serving officer, in the Royal Navy, and he still holds senior rank in all three branches of the services, including Commandant-in-Chief of the Royal Marines. It was partly through his influence that Prince Edward joined the Royal Marines but during his training period he decided that a service life was not for him and he resigned.

The Queen's second son, the Duke of York, is still serving in the Royal Navy having seen action in the Falkland Islands Campaign as a helicopter pilot in 1983, while Prince Charles, who is Colonel-in-Chief of six regiments, qualified for his 'wings' as a pilot in the RAF. He then transferred to the Royal Navy where he subsequently commanded his own ship HMS *Bronington*.

While all the ladies in the Royal Family enjoy close ties with various regiments and service units throughout the Commonwealth, the Princess Royal is the only one with a uniformed appointment. This came about when she was asked to become Chief Commandant of the Women's Royal Naval Service (WRNS). She is also Colonel-in-Chief of no fewer

than 11 regiments in the United Kingdom, Canada, Australia and New Zealand. Princess Alexandra, The Queen's cousin, is associated with 11 service units also, including The Queen's Own Rifles of Canada, the Women's Royal Australian Naval Service and the Royal Hong Kong Police Force.

The Princess of Wales has regiments in Canada and Australia, while her first British regiments were the 13/18th Hussars and the Hampshires, all of whom keep her in touch with their activities. A favourite duty of the Queen Mother is to present shamrocks to the regiments of the Irish Guards on St Patrick's Day.

TOP LEFT: *The Queen meets paratroopers of the 5th Airborne Brigade on Salisbury Plain.*

TOP RIGHT: *Wearing the uniform of Chief Commandant of the WRNS, the Princess Royal makes an inspection of HMS* Royal Arthur.

ABOVE: *Prince Philip talks with Gurkhas in Hong Kong. He is Colonel-in-Chief of several Commonwealth regiments.*

# The Young Royals

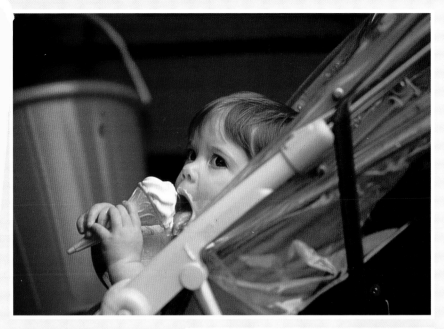

ABOVE: *Like all children, Princess Eugenie relishes an ice-cream.*

ABOVE RIGHT: *Peter and Zara Phillips, the children of the Princess Royal, are helping out at a sporting event held in the grounds of their home at Gatcombe Park.*

RIGHT: *Full of fun, Princess Beatrice plays hobbyhorse with a folded umbrella.*

OPPOSITE LEFT: *Prince Henry braves the ski slopes in Lech, Austria.*

OPPOSITE ABOVE RIGHT: *Prince William follows his family's fascination with horses. He himself was in the saddle by the age of three.*

OPPOSITE BELOW RIGHT: *Lady Sarah Armstrong-Jones and her brother, Viscount Linley, visiting the Great Wall of China. They accompanied their mother, Princess Margaret, on this tour.*

The Queen's six grandchildren constitute the newest generation of the Royal Family. The eldest is Peter Phillips, the Princess Royal's son, who was born on 15 November 1977. At the time of his birth he was fifth in line of succession to the throne and the first royal grandchild in 500 years to be born a commoner. He and his sister Zara, born 15 May 1981, both attend boarding school.

The Prince and Princess of Wales's first son Prince William was born on 21 June 1982 and his younger brother Prince Henry, known as Harry, came along two years later on 15 September 1984. Rather than receiving education at home according to royal tradition, the children went to nursery school in London and Prince William is now a boarder at a preparatory school. They have travelled with their parents on occasional overseas tours, for instance in October 1991 when they accompanied them to Canada. Prince William is gradually being trained for his future role as King, having already taken up some public engagements.

The Duke and Duchess of York have two daughters: Princess Beatrice was born on 8 August 1988 at the Portland Hospital in London and given the names Beatrice Elizabeth Mary at her christening in the Chapel Royal, St James's Palace, on 20 December 1988. Their second daughter, Princess Eugenie Victoria Helena, was born on 23 March 1990 and christened at Sandringham on 23 December 1990.

# At Home

The residences occupied by the Royal Family are divided into those The Queen uses in her official capacity, her private homes and the 'Grace and Favour' houses and apartments she lends to her relations.

Buckingham Palace is The Queen's London residence and it is also the centre of administration for the monarchy. So only a small part is used by The Queen herself. Her private apartments are on the first floor facing Green Park where the accommodation is comfortable rather than luxurious. A staff of nearly 200 works in the Palace but of these only a handful actually comes into regular contact with Her Majesty.

Weekends are spent at Windsor, the largest castle in Europe and a royal fortress since the days of William the Conqueror. The two private houses owned by The Queen are Balmoral Castle in Scotland,

OPPOSITE ABOVE: *Balmoral Castle, situated on the banks of the River Dee, was bought and extended by Queen Victoria and her husband, Prince Albert, in the mid-1840s. She described it as her 'dear paradise', and it is here that The Queen can relax throughout August and September.*

LEFT: *Protected from the stiff north-west breezes by high walls, the Queen Mother enjoys her delightfully informal gardens at the Castle of Mey. She discovered this romantic 16th-century castle at the northernmost tip of Scotland shortly after her husband's death and had it renovated. Apart from Clarence House, her other homes are Royal Lodge at Windsor, and Birkhall on the Balmoral estate.*

BELOW LEFT: *Prince Charles at his home, Highgrove House.*

where the interior is decorated in the bold colours of tartan including Royal Stuart, and Sandringham House in Norfolk, whose estate extends to 20,000 acres. It was The Queen's late father King George VI who once said, 'In London I have a house – in Sandringham I have a home.'

For the first five years of her marriage Her Majesty (then Princess Elizabeth) lived in Clarence House, now the home of Queen Elizabeth the Queen Mother. It is one of the most gracious houses in London with every room bearing the imprint of the Queen Mother's personality. Most of her staff have been with her for years and they are among the most loyal and happiest of all royal servants. Along with several other members of the Royal Family, the Prince and Princess of Wales live in Kensington Palace which has been divided into a number of elegant apartments. Other residents include Princess Margaret,

Princess Alice and the Duke and Duchess of Gloucester and Prince and Princess Michael of Kent. The Gloucesters have the biggest apartment, 35 rooms, while the Wales family occupy two apartments combined.

The Princess Royal's home is Gatcombe Park in what is described as Gloucestershire's royal triangle: Prince Charles owns nearby Highgrove House, with Prince Michael of Kent also close by.

OPPOSITE AND ABOVE: *The Princess of Wales has chosen pretty, feminine wallpapers for her homes. Family photographs help to create a personal, homely atmosphere. In the picture opposite she selects outfits with the help of David Emanuel. She is seen above at her desk in Kensington Palace.*

# Time Off

ABOVE: *T-shirts and shorts are appropriately casual for a restful holiday in Majorca. The Prince and Princess of Wales and their two children, the Princes William and Henry, soak up the sun on deck with their hosts King Juan Carlos and Queen Sofia of Spain and members of their family.*

Between them members of the Royal Family take part in a wide variety of activities during their spare time. They are all keen on sport and if horses figure largely in the overall picture it is perfectly understandable. The pursuit of equestrian excellence has been associated with royalty for centuries. The Queen, like all her family, grew up with horses and she cannot remember a time when she could not ride. Her main passion, however, is for horse-racing, a love she shares with her mother. They are both successful and enthusiastic racehorse owners but while the Queen Mother prefers hurdlers and steeplechasers, her daughter likes the sheer speed required for the flat. She has one

ambition left and that is for one of her horses to win the Derby, an accomplishment achieved three times by her great-grandfather King Edward VII.

The most successful sporting competitor in the family is the Princess Royal who became the European Three-Day Event Champion in 1971 riding The Queen's horse Doublet. She also represented Britain at the 1976 Olympic Games in Canada and ten years later rode her first winner as a lady jockey.

Polo has been a firm royal favourite for many years with first Prince Philip competing successfully, before arthritis forced him to retire and concentrate on his other equestrian pursuit, carriage driving,

and then Prince Charles, who plays regularly at Smith's Lawn, Windsor. His Royal Highness suffered a serious injury to his arm in 1990 while playing in a match, but he recovered and returned to the polo field the following season. A quieter pastime is painting and a book of his watercolours has been published, while he says his idea of a perfect evening is to sit in his study with an opera playing at full volume on his stereo system. The Prince and Princess of Wales and their children are all keen skiers and every year they spend a short holiday on the slopes. The Princess of Wales loves watching and playing tennis, and she swims regularly in the Buckingham Palace pool.

ABOVE: *Control of a team of horses or ponies is a skill that delights Prince Philip. He has represented England in international driving championships and generally attends the Royal Windsor Horse Show and other major events.*

LEFT: *Formerly an exclusively male preserve, racing on the flat now has a champion woman jockey in the Princess Royal. She is competing here at Sandown Park.*

27

BELOW: *Prince Charles is willing to have a go at anything. Here he tries his hand at sailboarding.*

TOP RIGHT: *The historic game of 'real' (royal) tennis appealed to Prince Edward. He is able to play on the court built by Henry VIII at Hampton Court Palace.*

CENTRE RIGHT: *Prince Charles tending his herb garden in the peace of Highgrove.*

RIGHT: *Princess Beatrice enthuses about the Windsor Horse Show as much as her grandmother. The Queen is also a keen photographer.*

As old as the century, the Queen Mother is still amazingly active. She has often shared her love of fishing with one of her grandchildren; both Prince Edward and Prince Charles are enthusiastic about the sport. Today there is nothing she likes better than a stroll with her dogs, or a little gentle gardening.

The Duke of York, who in his younger days played rugby, has more recently turned to the pastime of golf. He continues his lifelong interest in photography and has exhibited a number of his photographs. However, it is Prince Edward who has returned to a sport that is truly royal. He plays 'real' (or royal) tennis, on indoor courts at Hampton Court Palace where, in the 16th century, his ancestor King Henry VIII often enjoyed a game.